The UNIVERSE, BLACK HOLES and the BIG BANG

First published in 2015 by Wayland
© Wayland 2015

Wayland
Hachette Children's Books
338 Euston Road
London NW1 3BH

Wayland Australia
Level 17/207 Kent Street
Sydney, NSW 2000

Produced by White-Thomson Publishing Ltd.

White-Thomson Publishing Ltd
www.wtpub.co.uk
+44 (0) 843 208 7460

Editor: Izzi Howell
Cover design and concept: Lisa Peacock
Designer: Ian Winton

A catalogue for this title is available from the British Library

ISBN: 978 0 7502 9234 4

eBook ISBN: 978 0 7502 9235 1

Dewey Number: 523.1-dc23

10 9 8 7 6 5 4 3 2 1

MIX
Paper from
responsible sources
FSC
www.fsc.org
FSC® C104740

Wayland is a division of Hachette Children's Books,
an Hachette UK company.

www.hachette.co.uk

The website addresses (URLs) included in this book were valid at the time of going to press. However, because of the nature of the Internet, it is possible that some addresses may have changed, or sites may have changed or closed down since publication. While the author and publisher regret any inconvenience this may cause the readers, no responsibility for any such changes can be accepted by either the author or the publisher.

Picture credits
Shutterstock/Vladimir Arndt cover (background), NASA/JPL-Caltech/Univ. of Ariz. cover (tl), Shutterstock/Antony McAulay cover (cr), Shutterstock/Lonely cover (bl), Shutterstock/jupeart cover (br), Shutterstock/Petrafler cover (br), Shutterstock/A-R-T title page (background), Shutterstock/Kotse title page (b). NASA / WMAP Science Team 4, Shutterstock/RATOCA 5 (cr), Shutterstock/RedKoala 5 (bl), Thinkstock/Kanomdesign 5 (br), Science Photo Library/Mikkel Juul Jensen 6 (tl), Thinkstock/joaquin croxatto 6 (bl), Shutterstock/bioraven 7 (bl), Illustris Collaboration/Illustris Simulation 7 (br), Wikimedia 8 (tr), NASA / WMAP Science Team 8 (bl), Shutterstock/abstractdesignlabs 9 (tr), Shutterstock/bioraven 9 (cr), Dreamstime/ Thomas Jurkowski 9 (b), Science Photo Library/Mark Garlick 10-11, Stefan Chabluk 12 (including designs from Shutterstock/Macrovector and Shutterstock/veronchick84), Shutterstock/MW47 13 (bl), Shutterstock/Brent Hofacker 13 (br), ESA/NASA/Hubble 14 (tl), Wikimedia/Andrew Z. Colvin 14 (tc), NASA/JPL 14 (tr), A. Nota (ESA/STScI) et al., ESA, NASA 14 (bl), NASA/JPL-Caltech 14 (br), NASA, ESA, and the Hubble SM4 ERO Team 15 (tc), Shutterstock/RedKoala 15 (br), Science Photo Library/Mark Garlick 16, Shutterstock/RedKoala 17 (tr), NASA/JPL-Caltech 17 (tr), NASA/JPL-Caltech 18 (tl), NASA/CXC/M.Weiss 18 (br), Shutterstock/radmilla75 19 (cl), X-ray NASA/CXC/MIT/C.Canizares, M.Nowak; Optical NASA/STScI 19 (cr), X-ray: NASA/CXC/SAO; Optical: Rolf Olsen; Infrared: NASA/JPL-Caltech 20, Shutterstock/Skocko 21 (tr), Shutterstock/MichaelTaylor 21 (c), Shutterstock/sakkmesterke 22, Science Photo Library 23, NASA 24 (tl), NASA/JPL-Caltech 24 (bl), Shutterstock/RedKoala 24 (br), Shutterstock/Virinaflora 25 (cl), NASA, ESA, W. Keel (Univ. Alabama), et al., Galaxy Zoo Team 25 (cl), NASA 26 (tl), Shutterstock/bioraven 26 (br), NASA Ames/SETI Institute/JPL-Caltech 27 (tr), Shutterstock/RATOCA 27 (bl), NASA / WMAP Science Team 28, Shutterstock/Designua 29 (tr), Shutterstock/antishock 29 (bl), Shutterstock/bioraven 29 (br).

Design elements throughout: Shutterstock/Aphelleon, Shutterstock/PinkPueblo, Shutterstock/topform, Shutterstock/Nikiteev_Konstantin, Shutterstock/Elinalee, Shutterstock/mhatzapa, Shutterstock/notkoo, Shutterstock/Hilch. Shutterstock/CPdesign, Shutterstock/antoninaart.

CONTENTS

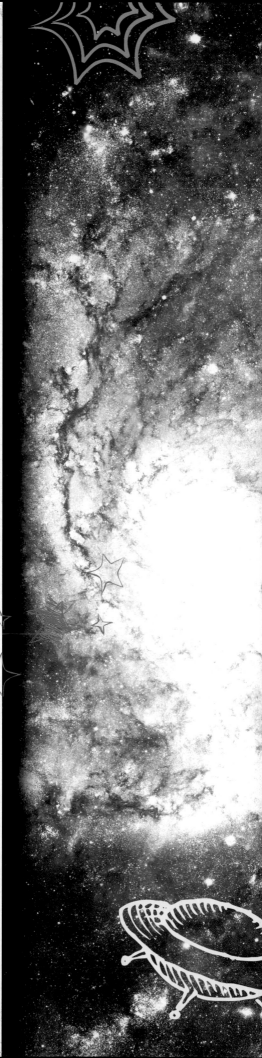

WHAT IS THE UNIVERSE?

The universe consists of absolutely everything we can see or sense, from the tiny particles inside an atom to giant galaxies that take light millions of years to cross.

Ancient Age

Cosmologists estimate that the universe is approximately 13.7 billion years old. This is a mind-blowingly long period of time. Humans are latecomers to the party, with our species, homo sapiens, evolving on Earth just 200,000 years ago.

The WMAP satellite helped to measure the age of the universe.

LOCAL LONG DISTANCE

To get an idea of the scale of the universe, you can work up from distances in the solar system. One Astronomical Unit (AU) is equal to the average distance between the Sun and Earth – 149.6 million km. The furthest human-made object from Earth is the Voyager I space probe, which is 130 AU away and only just leaving the solar system.

THINKING BIGGER...

To measure larger distances, scientists use light years. This is the distance that light travels in a year – a whopping 9,460,528,404,847 km. The nearest star to Earth, besides the Sun, is Proxima Centauri, which is approximately 271,000 AU or 4.24 light years away.

...AND BIGGER

It takes just 1.3 seconds for light to travel between the Moon and Earth. In contrast, it takes light 100,000 years to cross our home galaxy, the Milky Way. The Milky Way is just one of billions of galaxies, separated by millions of light years of space.

WHAT'S SPACE LIKE?

We imagine space as being empty, but it actually contains very thinly spread molecules of gas and dust. Space close to a star may be warmed up by the star's heat energy but it is seriously cold elsewhere, with an average temperature of -270.2 °C.

Shhhh!

In space no one can hear you scream ... or make any other sound for that matter. Sound travels in waves by making molecules of matter vibrate. In the large empty areas of space, there are very few molecules to vibrate, so there is just silence.

93 BILLION
THE NUMBER OF LIGHT YEARS THE OBSERVABLE UNIVERSE IS ESTIMATED TO MEASURE, ACCORDING TO THE EUROPEAN SPACE AGENCY (ESA).

INVESTIGATING THE UNIVERSE

Ptolemy's model
of the universe

In the past, many views on space were affected by religion. Recent scientific advances have helped us to learn a great deal about the universe and how it works.

Self-Centred

For over 1,500 years, many people agreed with the Egyptian scientist Ptolemy, who thought that Earth was the centre of the universe. This view was challenged by Islamic scholars in the Middle Ages and by the Polish astronomer Nicolaus Copernicus in 1543. Copernicus proposed that Earth and other planets travelled around the Sun, but he still placed the solar system at the centre of the universe.

Burning Issue

The Italian philosopher, Giordano Bruno was one of the first to state that the solar system was just one of many star systems in space. He also believed that people lived on other planets! His views brought him into conflict with the Church and in 1600, he was burned at the stake.

THINKING AHEAD

Many advances in astronomy were made without telescopes, simply by thinking things through. In 1687, Isaac Newton presented his theory of how gravity affects every object in the universe. 70 years later, Immanuel Kant suggested that the solar system formed from discs of spinning dust and gas.

Fuzzy Thinking

After telescopes were invented in the 17th century, astronomers discovered new objects in space – fuzzy spiral shapes containing pinpoints of bright light. These were originally called nebulae (meaning clouds), but science would later show that they were star-packed galaxies.

GALACTIC BREAKTHROUGH

Until the 20th century, most scientists thought that the Milky Way contained the entire universe. This changed when an American astronomer, Edwin Hubble, measured objects in the Andromeda Galaxy, using a giant 2.5-m telescope. He found that the objects were 10 times further away than the most distant stars in the Milky Way, thus proving that other galaxies exist.

Modern advances in technology have helped us to investigate space. The Illustris simulation, shown here, used 8,000 powerful computer chips to produce a model of how galaxies may have formed.

2,000

THE NUMBER OF YEARS IT WOULD TAKE A REGULAR PC TO MAKE ALL THE CALCULATIONS IN THE ILLUSTRIS SIMULATION OF THE UNIVERSE.

HOW THE UNIVERSE BEGAN

The Big Bang theory is the most commonly accepted idea of how the universe began. It states that the universe, and everything it now contains, emerged from a single point. Energy, matter and time simply did not exist before – there was no 'before' the Big Bang.

Coming Up With The Big Bang

Discoveries in the early 20th century showed that galaxies were moving away from each other, which meant that the universe was expanding. Georges Lemaître suggested that if the universe was increasing in size, it must therefore have been smaller in the past. This led him to conclude that the universe began out of a single point. His ideas, published in 1927–31, formed the basis of the Big Bang theory.

Georges Lemaître (1894–1966) was a Belgian priest and scientist.

This photo shows the cosmic background radiation present 375,000 years after the Big Bang. Hot spots are red, cold spots are dark blue.

IN THE BACKGROUND

The Big Bang theory states that after the Big Bang, cosmic energy travelled through the young universe, before cooling and fading into the background. This idea is supported by scientific evidence, as cosmic background radiation is the oldest energy that scientists are able to observe.

Pigeon Poop

Two young scientists, Robert Wilson and Arno Penzias, were the first to discover cosmic background radiation, in 1964. While cleaning out a radio antenna dish that was full of pigeons and pigeon droppings, they detected low-level radio noise. This proved to be background radiation from the Big Bang.

MODELLING THE MOMENT

We cannot look back at the very start of the Big Bang, so our theories come from mathematical models and experiments, such as the Large Hadron Collider (LHC). The LHC whizzes particles of atoms down a 27-km-long tunnel at almost the speed of light, crashing them into each other to simulate the conditions shortly after the Big Bang.

3.7 BILLION
THE COST IN POUNDS OF BUILDING THE LARGE HADRON COLLIDER.

the Large Hadron Collider

DEVELOPMENT AND FORMATION

Strap yourself in. You're about to go on the wildest ride imaginable, starting at the very beginning of the universe.

Not Exactly A Bang

The universe didn't explode, but rather expanded — at a truly incredible rate. Scientists estimate that in a tiny fraction of a second, it went from something smaller than an atom to something bigger than an entire galaxy. It continued to grow to trillions and trillions of its original size.

WHEN DID THE FIRST GALAXIES FORM?

No one is certain. It was once thought that galaxies didn't form for the first billion years. But, in 2011, the Hubble Space Telescope discovered the oldest known galaxy, estimated to have formed around 500 million years after the Big Bang.

The Formation Of The Universe

In the briefest of moments, the universe expanded at an amazing rate. Just after the Big Bang, the universe was so hot that any particles that managed to form were instantly destroyed.

380,000 years

After around 380,000 years, the universe had cooled down to about 3,000 °C. Hydrogen and helium atoms managed to form. The universe continued to expand but not as rapidly as before.

400 million years

From around 400,000 years to about 400 million years after the Big Bang, the universe was a dark, foggy place.

Around 400 million years after the Big Bang, the first protostars formed. Eventually, these protostars began to carry out nuclear fusion in their cores and started shining brightly.

9 billion years

Our solar system was created around 4.6 billion years ago, more than 9 billion years after the Big Bang. First, the Sun formed from a large cloud of gas and dust. As it developed, a large disc of leftover gas and dust grew around it, eventually creating the planets and other parts of the solar system.

13.7 billion years (present day)

In 1929, Edwin Hubble discovered something fundamental about the universe: it was still expanding! This breakthrough reinforced the Big Bang theory and has been studied by scientists ever since.

Redshift

Remember the last time a police car drove past you with its siren blaring? The sound is higher pitched as it travels towards you and lower pitched as it drives away. This is called the Doppler effect. A similar thing happens with light, known as redshift.

EDWIN'S WIN-WIN

Hubble worked out that galaxies were moving away from the solar system by measuring distances and using redshift. He found that the further a galaxy lay from Earth, the faster it was moving away. The conclusion was that the entire universe was expanding.

When an object moves away, its light waves are stretched out and the object appears red – a redshift.

When an object in space moves towards you, its light waves are squeezed together and the object appears blue – a blueshift.

The Hubble Constant

Hubble estimated the speed at which the universe was expanding, known as the Hubble constant. Today the Hubble constant is thought to be around 71 km/s for every 3.26 million light years (mly) a galaxy lies away from us.

WHAT'S THE UNIVERSE EXPANDING INTO?

It isn't expanding into anything. Space within the universe is expanding, getting bigger between the galaxies. It is a bit like making chocolate chip cookies. The chips (galaxies) start close to each other but as the cookies are baked and expand, the chips move away from each other.

FURTHER AND FASTER

Because the universe is expanding, the further away a galaxy is, the faster it is moving. A galaxy 3.26 mly away from us is receding at a speed of 71 km/s. However, a galaxy 100 times further away (326 mly) is moving 100 times faster, giving it a speed of 7,100 km/s. Whoosh!

The way that cookies expand when they are baked is similar to the way that the universe is expanding.

13

GROUPS, CLUSTERS AND SUPERCLUSTERS

Gravity often pulls several galaxies together into groups. Large groups, made up of many galaxies, are called clusters. The number of galaxies in a cluster can range from a handful to several thousands.

The Local Group

The Milky Way is part of the Local Group, a collection of over 30 galaxies. Andromeda is the biggest galaxy in the Local Group, containing more than twice the number of stars found in the Milky Way. At the other end of the scale is the Ursa Minor Dwarf, which is less than 10 light years across but contains many ancient stars.

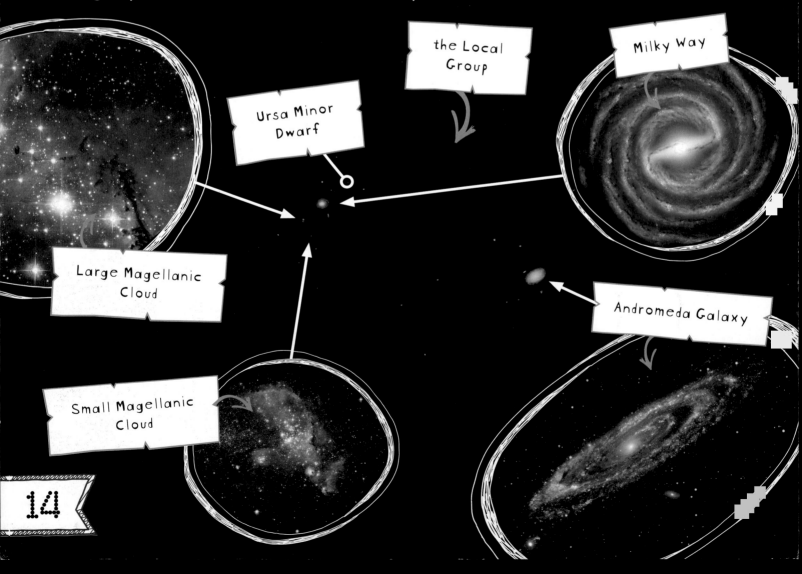

the Local Group

Milky Way

Ursa Minor Dwarf

Large Magellanic Cloud

Andromeda Galaxy

Small Magellanic Cloud

Neighbouring Clusters

The largest nearby cluster of galaxies is the Virgo Cluster, which covers an area of approximately 10 million light years and contains around 160 large galaxies, including the giant elliptical galaxy M87.

COLLIDING CLUSTER

One of the smallest clusters contains just five galaxies. Stephan's Quintet is about 280 million light years away from us. Four of its five galaxies are locked in a gigantic collision, creating a shock wave bigger in size than the Milky Way!

Two of the galaxies in Stephan's Quintet are so close that they look like one galaxy.

WHAT IS A SUPERCLUSTER?

A supercluster is a cluster of clusters. These can contain hundreds of galaxy clusters and are unimaginably vast. The Local Group, Virgo Cluster and around another 100 groups and clusters, are all part of the Laniakea Supercluster.

160 MILLION
THE DIAMETER IN LIGHT YEARS OF THE LANIAKEA SUPERCLUSTER.

BLACK HOLES

Mysterious, invisible objects that gobble up stars, planets and even galaxies, black holes are one of the most fascinating and terrifying features of the universe.

Super Dense

A black hole is anything but an empty hole. It is an area that packs a huge amount of material into a very small space, creating an unbelievably dense object. The more mass an object has, the more gravity it exerts on other objects, so a black hole has phenomenal gravity, pulling everything into itself.

STELLAR BLACK HOLES

Stellar black holes start out as large stars, which are ripped apart by a giant explosion called a supernova. After the explosion, the core of the star collapses in on itself. If the core has enough mass, then gravity will keep on pulling in on itself until a black hole is formed.

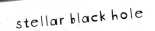
stellar black hole

Accretion disc — matter often forms a spinning disc around a black hole as it is drawn towards it.

Event horizon — the point of no return for matter drawn towards a black hole.

Singularity — the entire mass of a black hole is contained within a single point in space.

On The Horizon

You don't want to be anywhere near a black hole's event horizon. This is the boundary line that marks a region of space around a black hole, from which nothing can escape. Everything within the event horizon, from the smallest dust particles to entire stars, will be drawn into the black hole and pulverised by its extreme gravity.

24,000
THE NUMBER OF LIGHT YEARS FROM EARTH THAT THE NEAREST KNOWN BLACK HOLE, SAGITTARIUS A*, LIES.

The black hole at the centre of the NGC 1097 galaxy has a mass 100 million times larger than that of the Sun.

black hole

SUPERMASSIVE BLACK HOLES

Supermassive black holes have far greater mass than stellar black holes. Scientists are unsure how they form, but they believe that most galaxies have a supermassive black hole at their centre. The black hole at the centre of the Milky Way galaxy is called Sagittarius A*. It has a mass equal to about 4.3 million Suns.

17

BLACK-HOLE HUNTERS

Astronomers seek out black holes in a number of ways. They look for gaps where something should be, observe the behaviour of stars and other bodies, and use instruments that can detect X-rays given off by matter near black holes.

Launched in 2012, NuSTAR is the first telescope in space that can focus X-rays into sharp images.

Tell-Tale Signs

Black-hole hunters keep their eyes peeled for visible objects in space behaving as if a giant object were nearby. This could be a star wobbling as it travels through space or a spinning disc of matter around an invisible centre.

HDE 226868

BLACK HOLE: CONFIRMED!

The first black hole to be discovered and confirmed was Cygnus X-1, about 10,000 light years from Earth. X-rays given off by Cygnus X-1 were spotted by the first dedicated X-ray telescope in space, NASA's Uhuru, in 1971.

Cygnus X-1 is dragging in material from the nearby star HDE 226868.

Double Trouble

A small number of galaxies, such as NGC 6240, have not one, but two supermassive black holes at their centre. Astronomers believe that this occurs when two galaxies merge into one. Despite their huge mass, the black holes orbit each other at speeds of up to 8 million km/h.

BIG THINGS IN SMALL PLACES

Giant black holes can also exist in small galaxies. M60-UCD1 is a dwarf galaxy with a tiny diameter of just 300 light years. Yet in 2014, the Hubble Space Telescope discovered a monstrous black hole at its centre, with the mass of 20 million Suns.

Give Us A Tune

A black hole found in the Perseus galaxy cluster has been sounding out the lowest note in the universe – a B flat, 57 octaves below a middle C!

HOW BIG IS THE BIGGEST SUPERMASSIVE BLACK HOLE?

The largest one found so far is a truly gigantic supermassive black hole at the centre of the NGC 4889 galaxy, with a mass equal to about 21 billion Suns!

supermassive black holes

Eventually, NGC 6240's two supermassive black holes will probably merge into one.

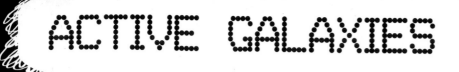

ACTIVE GALAXIES

The light that astronomers observe from regular galaxies, such as Andromeda, comes from stars within the galaxy. Active galaxies are different. They generate energy in tiny areas near their centres, known as galactic nuclei.

Not Jet Set

Scientists think that all active galaxies are 'powered' by black holes at their centre. In some active galaxies, known as radio galaxies, these black holes don't just pull in matter, they also spit out large jets of material at superfast speeds. This material cools down in space, forming enormous plumes of gas.

GIANT PLUMES

Centaurus A is a huge, elliptical radio galaxy, formed when two galaxies merged millions of years ago. It's around 12 million light years away, but it is the fifth-brightest galaxy in the night sky viewed from Earth. Its two giant jets are over a million light years long.

Centaurus A

Quasars

Quasars are extremely bright objects found in distant galaxies. Many are located 9–12 billion light years away, yet they can be studied on Earth because they emit vast amounts of energy, much of it as visible light.

Quasars are like pocket torches that can shine as bright as a whole city, drowning out the light from the other stars in their galaxy.

4 TRILLION

THE NUMBER OF TIMES MORE BRIGHTLY THAN THE SUN THAT THE 3C 273 QUASAR SHINES. IT WAS THE FIRST QUASAR TO BE DISCOVERED, IN THE 1960S.

IT'S HUGE!

A stunning cluster of 73 quasars has been discovered, around 9 billion light years from us. Called the Huge Large Quasar Group, it is so big that it would take light 4 billion years to travel across it. Some scientists believe it to be the largest structure in the universe.

DARK MATTER AND DARK ENERGY

Astronomers have learned much about the universe, but many questions remain unanswered. Two of the biggest questions concern things that we have not yet been able to observe – the deeply mysterious dark matter and dark energy.

A Dark-Matter Mystery

Scientists don't think that there's enough regular matter to explain the amount of gravity present in the universe. This suggests that the universe must contain a different type of matter that doesn't absorb or give out light or other waves, making it invisible. This is known as dark matter and it is thought to make up more than 80% of all the matter in the universe.

WHAT IS MATTER?

Matter is formed of atoms and makes up everything you can taste, touch and see, from a tube of toothpaste to a giant star. All objects made of matter exert gravity on other objects.

This is an artist's impression of what dark matter might look like, if we could see it.

WIMP!

What could dark matter be? One theory is Weakly Interacting Massive Particles (WIMPs) – particles that could pass through ordinary matter without any effect. If they were present everywhere throughout the universe, they might, all together, add up to the missing amount of matter. However, all experiments to find WIMPs have been unsuccessful so far.

One WIMP experiment placed a detector filled with low-pressure gas 1,100 m underground in a mine. The higher layers of rock absorbed other rays from the universe but scientists thought that WIMPs might pass through the rock into the detector, where they might collide with the gas particles. Unfortunately, no WIMPs were detected.

DARK ENERGY

In the 1990s, scientists discovered that the universe is expanding at a quicker rate than in the past. As gravity draws objects towards each other, they concluded that some force must be overcoming gravity and powering this increase in expansion speed. This unknown energy is called dark energy and remains a massive mystery.

other rays from the universe

rock

Possible path of WIMPs

rays absorbed by the rock

mine

WIMP detector

ODDITIES OF THE UNIVERSE

Dark matter and dark energy are not the only weird things found in the universe. Check out this collection of seriously strange bodies and phenomena that surprise and mystify scientists.

Quake!

Magnetars, a type of large neutron star, are responsible for earthquake-like tremors in space, known as starquakes. In 2004, a starquake from SGR 1806-20 was so powerful that some of its effects reached Earth's atmosphere, from over 50,000 light years away.

starquake

SGR 1806-20's starquake lasted less than a second, yet released more energy than the Sun releases in 100,000 years!

A TRUE SHOOTING STAR

What we call shooting stars are meteoroids – small pieces of rock or metal that burn up in Earth's atmosphere. One real star, though, is shooting through space at the incredibly high speed of 130 km/s. Mira is around the same size as the Sun, but it is getting smaller because it loses gas as it whizzes through space.

Mira is the only known star with a long tail.

13

THE LENGTH OF MIRA'S TAIL IN LIGHT YEARS.

Green Gas

In 2007, a Dutch schoolteacher, Hanny van Arkel discovered a strange, glowing, blue-green blob of gas floating in space close to a spiral galaxy. Named Hanny's Voorwerp (meaning Hanny's object), this is no small cloud. It's roughly the size of the Milky Way!

spiral galaxy

Hanny's Voorwerp

Fruit Loopy

Scientists have discovered a dust and gas cloud around 26,000 light years away, called Sagittarius B2. This cloud is full of ethyl formate, the chemical that gives raspberries their fruity flavour.

WATER, WATER

The universe's biggest known reservoir of water is not found on Earth, but around a quasar over 12 billion light years away. The APM 08279+5255 quasar is surrounded by a giant disc of water vapour that contains 140 billion times more water than Earth's oceans!

IS THERE ANYONE OUT THERE?

The universe is unimaginably vast – can Earth really be the only place where intelligent life exists? Whilst no signs of extraterrestrial life have been found so far, some scientists remain hopeful that contact will be made one day.

A Message From Earth

With other star systems too far away for human spaceflight, scientists have tried different ways of making contact. The Pioneer 10 and 11 space probes carried gold plaques showing pictures of a naked man and woman, a simple map of the solar system, and the location of our solar system in the Milky Way.

The Voyager gold record is engraved with information about how to play the disc.

GOING FOR GOLD

The Voyager 1 and 2 space probes carried gold records containing sounds from Earth, as well as spoken greetings in 55 different languages. The probes are now the furthest machines from Earth; Voyager 1 has left the solar system and is now over 19 billion km away.

2 MILLION
THE NUMBER OF YEARS IT WILL TAKE PIONEER 10 TO GET CLOSE TO THE NEXT STAR IN ITS PATH, THE STAR ALDEBARAN.

New Worlds

Advances in astronomy have led to the discovery of over 1,800 planets orbiting stars other than the Sun. Some exoplanets may orbit their star at the right distance for liquid water to be present and for life to flourish.

Kepler-186f is the first Earth-sized planet to be found orbiting a star at a distance at which liquid water might be present on the planet's surface.

LISTENING IN

Instead of sending out signals, some alien-hunting projects scan the skies for signals from intelligent life outside the solar system. The Allen Telescope Array is a series of 42 radio telescopes that work together to seek out radio signals from deep space.

WHAT WAS THE ARECIBO MESSAGE?

In 1974, a message was beamed out in radio waves from the Arecibo radio telescope dish towards a cluster of stars about 21,000 light years away. The radio message shows simple block pictures of the Arecibo dish, our solar system and the key chemicals that make life possible on Earth.

Hi!

In 1967, researcher Jocelyn Bell discovered regular radio signals from space. She named the signals LGM-1, short for Little Green Men, but instead of coming from aliens, the signals came from the first pulsar star to be discovered.

HOW WILL IT ALL END?

First of all, relax. The universe probably has trillions of years to go before it ends, if it ever does. Cosmologists puzzle over what the distant future holds for the universe and have developed a number of theories.

Chilled Out

The Big Chill theory suggests that if the universe continued to expand forever, the void between galaxies would grow until they became lonely islands in space. The galaxies would run out of gas to make new stars and existing stars would eventually use up their energy and die. The universe would end up as a cold, dark wasteland.

WHAT SHAPE IS THE UNIVERSE?

No one knows. Various shapes have been proposed from a curved saddle-like shape to a sphere and even a ring doughnut! Cosmologists wonder whether the universe is infinite, meaning it continues forever, or whether it is finite and has a definite shape.

The universe's shape, and whether it is finite or infinite, might determine how it ends, if at all.

THE BIG RIP

In 2003, a new idea for how the universe might end was published. It suggested that the universe will keep on getting bigger, but at a faster and faster rate. As the universe expands more and more rapidly, it will overcome the gravity that holds everything together, ripping all matter apart.

The Big Crunch

An alternative ending for the universe sees it stop expanding at a moment in the very distant future. At that point, the force of gravity overcomes the force of expansion and begins pulling everything together. Galaxies would speed towards each other, colliding and merging as the universe shrinks. Eventually, it would collapse and fall inwards on itself to a single point.

the present universe

time

the big crunch

BOUNCING BACK

The Big Crunch might not be the end of the story, though. From that single point, it might be possible for a new Big Bang to cause another, quite different universe to emerge. This idea is known as the Big Bounce.

The Big Crunch might be like the Big Bang but in reverse. Scientists currently think that there needs to be a lot more matter in the universe for the Big Crunch to be the likely ending.

the Big Bounce theory

The universe gets to a single point.

The universe starts to collapse.

A new universe starts to expand.

29

GLOSSARY

accretion disc – a disc of matter that may build up around a very dense object such as a black hole.

atom – the smallest unit of a chemical element.

Big Bang – the theory of how the universe formed out of a single point around 13.7 billion years ago.

billion – a thousand million.

black hole – an object in space with such strong gravity that nothing nearby can escape its pull, including light.

cosmic background radiation – radiation thought to have originated shortly after the Big Bang.

event horizon – the point beyond which nothing – not even light – can escape the gravity of a black hole.

gravity – the invisible force of attraction between objects.

light year – the distance travelled by light in a year (approximately 9.6 trillion km).

mass – how much matter an object contains.

matter – physical things that exist in space as solids, liquids or gases.

redshift – the stretching of light from an object, such as a galaxy, that is moving away from us.

speed of light – the speed at which light travels through space, approximately 299,792 km per second.

supermassive black hole – a black hole often found in the centre of a galaxy with a mass that may be equal to millions of Suns.

trillion – a million million.

FURTHER INFORMATION

Books

Science FAQs: Why Are Black Holes Black?
by Thomas Canavan (Franklin Watts, 2013)

The Story of Space: Looking Beyond
by Steve Parker (Franklin Watts, 2015)

World in Infographics: Space
by Jon Richards and Ed Simkins (Wayland, 2013)

Websites

http://www.schoolsobservatory.org.uk/astro/cosmos
Questions about space answered by scientists at the
National Schools' Observatory.

http://school.discoveryeducation.com/
schooladventures/Universe
An interesting look at aspects of the universe, how it
was formed and measuring distances in light years.

http://hubblesite.org/hubble_discoveries/dark_energy
A web presentation from the Hubble Space Telescope
team explaining how scientists first encountered the
mystery of dark energy.

INDEX

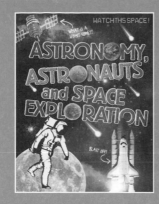

978 0 7502 9228 3

Stargazing
Optical Telescopes
Observatories
Seeing Other Waves
Radio Astronomy
Observatories in Space
Lift Off!
Space Probes
Landers and Rovers
Spacemen and Women
Astronaut Training
The International Space Station
Life in Space

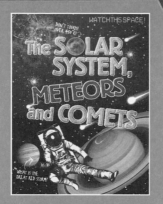

978 0 7502 9231 3

Meet the Neighbours
What's a Planet, What's a Moon?
Planet Earth
The Moon and its Orbit
Mercury and Venus: Strange Neighbours
Mars: the Red Planet
Jupiter: it's Massive
Saturn: Lord of the Rings
Uranus and Neptune
Asteroids and Dwarf Planets
Meteors and Meteorites
Comets
Exoplanets

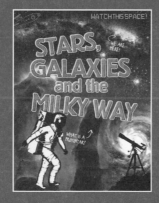

978 0 7502 9225 2

Starry Skies
Our Nearest Star
A Protostar is Born
Main Sequence Stars
Seeing Stars
Star Quality
Strange Stars
Star Death
Supernova!
Neutron Stars and Pulsars
Galaxies
Galaxy Types
The Milky Way

978 0 7502 9234 4

What is the Universe?
Investigating the Universe
How the Universe Began
Development and Formation
The Expanding Universe
Groups, Clusters and Superclusters
Black Holes
Black-Hole Hunters
Active Galaxies
Dark Matter and Dark Energy
Oddities of the Universe
Is there Anyone out there?
How Will it all End?